PAULA REGO

TALES FROM THE NATIONAL GALLERY

D1471483

Essays by
Germaine Greer and Colin Wiggins

National Gallery Publications Limited

Exhibition dates

25 April-1 June 1991
Plymouth City Museum and Art Gallery

15 June-20 July 1991
Middlesbrough Art Gallery

3 August-25 September 1991
Whitworth Art Gallery, Manchester

22 October -30 November 1991
Cooper Art Gallery, Barnsley

13 December 1991-29 February 1992
The National Gallery, London

Published in Great Britain in 1991 by
National Gallery Publications Limited
5/6 Pall Mall East, London SW1Y 5BA

British Library Cataloguing in Publication Data
Rego, Paula
Paula, Rego.
1. Portugal
I. Title   II. Greer, Germaine, *1939 -*   III. Wiggins, Colin
759.69

ISBN 0-947645-96-9

Designed by Joe Swift
Printed and bound in Great Britain by White Dove Press

Front cover: *Time - Past and Present* by Paula Rego.
Back cover: Paula Rego, photograph by Colin Harvey

Sponsor's Preface

FOR more than fifty years we have been providers of industrial and commercial premises assisting economic revival in areas of England affected by urban or rural decline.

In the 1990s and beyond our aim is to work alongside private investors and developers, continuing to ensure that properties are available for growing firms in the regions.

We recognise the need to enhance the lives of communities where we are active, and the importance placed on quality of life by businesses seeking to relocate and expand. With that in mind we have a substantial national programme to support and encourage the arts.

ENGLISH ESTATES

Head Office: St George's House, Kingsway, Team Valley, Gateshead, Tyne & Wear, NE11 0NA. Tel: (091) 487 8941. Fax: (091) 487 5690.

Offices at: Ashbourne, Cockermouth, Consett, Chatham, Gateshead, Norwich, Sleaford, Hereford, Thornaby, Truro, Plymouth, Yeovil.

Foreword

FROM its beginning in 1824 the National Gallery has always been closely involved with contemporary artists. It is traditional, for example, that there should be a practising artist on the Board of Trustees – a position first held by Sir Thomas Lawrence and currently by Euan Uglow. In recent years this association between an Old Master collection and contemporary art has become a pivotal part of the Gallery's public life, with the *Artist's Eye* exhibitions, selected by senior artists, and the Artist-in-Residence scheme, whereby a younger artist was given a studio on the premises, which was opened to the public each week.

The appointment of the first National Gallery Associate Artist is another expression of this continuing relationship between the old and the new. The brief to the appointed artist is to produce during the term of their appointment work directly related to paintings in the Collection.

Accordingly, we were delighted when Paula Rego accepted our invitation to initiate this new venture. We were even more delighted at her superbly imaginative response to that brief. Visitors to this exhibition will surely understand why and, we hope, be able to share in that delight. Paula's work is a firm reminder that art continues to be made today and did not suddenly stop, as the artificial barrier that causes the National Gallery's Collection to end at the early part of this century may sometimes suggest. Additionally, Paula has conclusively demonstrated that continuing relevance of an Old Master collection to artists working today.

This association would not have happened without the support of English Estates. It is through their generosity that the exhibition is able to travel and therefore be seen by a wider public. Uniquely for a National Gallery sponsor, English Estates have not simply supported an exhibition, but have played a key part in the initiation of new art, and to them go our heartfelt thanks.

Neil MacGregor
Director

Philippe de Champaigne, *The Vision of Saint Joseph*, *c*. 1638.
Canvas, 209 x 155.5 cm.

Tales from The National Gallery

Colin Wiggins

THE seventeenth-century French artist Philippe de Champaigne painted his *Vision of Saint Joseph* for a church in Paris that has since been demolished. In his picture the angel of the Lord appears to the sleeping Saint Joseph, revealing to him that the Virgin Mary is pregnant by the Holy Spirit. The tools of his carpenter's trade are scattered carelessly about him, telling us that Joseph is experiencing this revelation while in a sudden divinely induced sleep that has caught him unawares. In contrast, the wide-awake Virgin looks up from her reading, her sewing tools neatly tidied away under her table.

This was one of the paintings used by Paula Rego during her term as the first National Gallery Associate Artist. Part of the Associate Artist's brief is that he or she should make direct use of the paintings in the Collection, and Paula's *Joseph's Dream* was the last of the large-scale works to be completed for this exhibition, providing a climax to the gradual but evident influence that working in a major collection of Old Master paintings has had on the artist.

Paula's picture shows a version of Philippe de Champaigne's *Vision of Saint Joseph* as a work in progress, being painted by a

Joseph's Dream.
Acrylic on paper laid on canvas,
183 x 132 cm.

young woman artist. She sits on a small folding stool, the legs of which seem to creak under her weight as her ample bottom and thighs appear to thrust out of the picture space. Scattered carelessly beside her, like Saint Joseph's tools in Champaigne's painting, are her working drawings, one of which shows the preceding biblical event, the Annunciation to Mary. The young woman artist gazes intently at the figure of a man slumped in a deep sleep, and incorporates him into her painting, where he plays the part of Saint Joseph. In Paula's painting there is a wonderful blurring of the boundaries between what is 'real' and what is painted. The scene that we see, that of a picture being painted, is set in our own time and is therefore 'real'. The figures in the young woman's picture are of course painted, but the angel seems so solid that he might be understood as hovering directly above the woman's head, not necessarily part of her painting at all but in the room with her, perhaps providing her with some kind of artistic inspiration as she labours in what, after all, is a man's world.

The subject of artist and model is a common one in the history of art, but usually the role of the artist is played by a man and his model is a woman. Here the roles are reversed. The angel is on the side of the woman, and the heaviness of the man's pose perhaps indicates that his sleep, like that of Saint Joseph, is also divinely induced. As certain primitive peoples are said to be afraid of being photographed in case their spirits are captured, so the act of being painted by this woman puts this man under

Studies on paper for *Joseph's Dream*.

her power. The young artist is acquiring power by the very act of painting the slumbering man. Paula's role as a woman artist is, of course, very much central to the meaning of this picture.

> ' I wanted to do a girl drawing a man very much, because this role reversal is interesting. She's getting power from doing this you see. And then I went upstairs and I saw Philippe de Champaigne's picture, which I'd never seen before, and the two things fused in some peculiar manner. That picture is so solid, the angel is so solid, and Saint Joseph is so solid. It's wonderful. '

The solidity of the characters in Champaigne's picture is undoubtedly one of its most remarkable features, and, similarly, of the four large paintings shown in this exhibition *Joseph's Dream* is the most weighty. Just as the angel, who at first glance appears to be a character in the woman's painting, seems to burst through into the room in which the artist sits, so too does the artist threaten to leave her world and burst through into ours. The strength of Paula's drawing, the stool's buckling legs and the perspective effects made by the sheets of drawings on the floor make us feel that at any moment this woman could lean back a little bit too far and topple out into our world.

Pinned up behind the sleeping man are some drawings of figures, who seem to flit across the wall. A dog appears to bite the ankle of one of the figures. Goya-like, these pictures seem like mysterious evocations of dreams or distant memories. There is also a rhino, but a rhino without a horn. What can this mean?

Perhaps the rhino is a punning reference to the bulky form of the sleeping man. Deprived of his horn, the rhino is deprived of his power; trapped in his deep sleep, so too is the man. It is the woman painter, guided by her angel, who has the power here.

The first painting in this exhibition is called *The Bullfighter's Godmother*. This was made before Paula took up her appointment as Associate Artist, but is included because it forms a pair with *The Fitting*, the first painting to be made at the Gallery. The bullfighter, a young man of about sixteen, is being prepared for his first bullfight by his godmother. The little girl who sits with his cape on her knees is Death's goddaughter. She is also helping him to get ready. The sinister, almost gleeful, expression on her face suggests the fate she is planning. The picture takes place in a hotel room in Madrid, in 1957, where Paula once stayed with Vic, her husband, who died in 1988.

When she had finished this painting Paula immediately started work on *The Fitting*.

'After I painted the red satin cape I decided that I wanted to paint a huge blue satin skirt. I wanted to paint this skirt very much, and I actually made one, a little model. I already had in mind the idea of doing a picture of a dressmaker, with a girl trying on a ballgown. When I decided to do this hotel room in Madrid I thought of a lot of characters who would all have rooms there, and in one of the rooms this would be taking place. There is a girl going to her first ball – both these paintings are initiation rites you see – and she'll be trying on this

Studies on paper for *The Bullfighter's Godmother*.

The Bullfighter's Godmother.
Acrylic on paper laid on canvas,
122 x 152.4 cm.

The Fitting.
Acrylic on paper laid on canvas,
132 x 183 cm.

Studies on paper for *The Fitting*.

ballgown. The dressmaker is kneeling beside the girl tacking up her hem, and the little girl on the chair is the dressmaker's daughter. She had polio as a child. In some of the drawings I put a brace on her legs but I decided not to in the painting because it would have been too melodramatic, and so I gave her Petrushka legs. The woman on the right is the girl's mother. '

The characters and scenes within Paula's paintings often have for her very specific identities and meanings. Of course, spectators of these pictures cannot hope to know these meanings unless they are told, but this is unimportant to Paula, who hopes that people will make up their own stories. 'The stories are all important to me, but I use them just to create a mood,' she says.

Indeed, we can experience Old Master paintings in much the same way. Philippe de Champaigne's *Vision of Saint Joseph* was painted for an audience that was already familiar with the story and its meaning. It was made for a church, to be seen by a Roman Catholic congregation. Now it hangs in an art gallery and its audience is undefined and unlimited – it is seen by literally thousands of visitors with a non-Christian background. Similarly, other National Gallery paintings, often with complex Christian or classical iconography, can baffle even the most erudite of scholars. But a lack of knowledge of its original meaning need not handicap our enjoyment of a painting and can even enhance the mystery. As Paula says, 'That's the wonderful thing about pictures, you can always make up your own story.'

But even if we know who the characters in *The Fitting* are, there are still mysteries to tease and tantalise, even to unnerve and disquieten us. As in the best fairy tales, Paula's paintings do not simply delight and entertain, they carry undercurrents of the nasty, the sinister and the frightening. The dressmaker's daughter, with her fragile broken body, will never know the delights of her first ball. She is relegated to the background and slumps, pathetically and pitiably, in marked contrast to the blooming fertility of the girl in the blue dress. This contrast is emphasised even more when we look at the girl's proud mother, overseeing her daughter's fitting with obvious delight. She is unaware of the monstrous overblown grotesquerie of her daughter, with her stupid unthinking expression. As with the young bullfighter in the previous picture, happiness surely cannot be in store for her. On the right, on top of a cracked piece of furniture, are a white tablecloth, two books and a candle-end. Is this perhaps a sacrificial altar? Carved in relief on the screen behind the figures are a mother and her young baby, who are under terrible threat from a frightening creature with a devil's head, who seems to want to steal the child. This creature, explains Paula, is the Devil's wife, but we do not need to know this in order to understand the dreadful implications of the scene.

The Fitting is significant in that it was the first painting that Paula completed at the National Gallery. She remembers how she felt on being invited to become Associate Artist:

Drawing after Jan Steen's *The Effects of Intemperance*.
Pen and ink on paper, 30 x 40 cm.

Jan Steen, *The Effects of Intemperance*, *c.* 1662-3.
Wood (oak), 76 x 106.5 cm.

Andrea Mantegna, *Samson and Delilah*, *c.* 1490.
Linen, 47 x 37 cm.

'I was very scared and a bit daunted! But to find one's way anywhere one has to find one's own door, just like Alice, you see. You take too much of one thing and you get too big, then you take too much of another and you get too small. You've got to find your own doorway into things . . . and I thought the only way you can get into things is, so to speak, through the basement . . . which is exactly where my studio is, in the basement! So I can creep upstairs and snatch at things, and bring them down with me to the basement, where I can munch away at them. And what I bring down here from upstairs varies a lot, but I always bring something back into my den. I'm a sort of poacher here, really, that's what I am. '

Before painting the girl's dress in *The Fitting*, Paula had looked closely at the girl's dress in Jan Steen's *The Effects of Intemperance*, and even made a small copy of the painting. More striking, however, is the way she has used the carving on the screen to add another layer to the narrative of her painting. This scene is employed in much the same way as Hogarth, in his *Marriage à La Mode*, used paintings within paintings to help tell the story, although the direct inspiration for the screen in *The Fitting* comes from Mantegna.

'I went and looked at the Mantegna paintings that are pretending to be made of stone and marble, like a kind of bas-relief, and although my relief is supposed to be carved out of wood, not stone, I got the idea from Mantegna. I steal things – I steal the stories, I steal animals, the look of this, the look of that, how somebody paints fur. But it's more than just poaching . . . I felt more of the buffoon, like the maids in the Genet play who dress up in their mistress's clothes while she's away. Like little girls putting on their mother's make-up and furs. I have in

Antonello da Messina, *Saint Jerome in his Study,* *c.* 1456.
Wood (lime), painted area 46 x 36 cm.

the past felt more at home with popular art, rather than High Art –
kitchen talk, gutsy and immediate. But of course, here, with High Art,
you're right in it, with the great mysteries of the pictures upstairs. I'm
totally ill-equipped to deal with this, as the enormity of feeling makes
my mind reel, with vertigo or something, so the only thing I can do is
take a bit here and a bit there and hope that the stories will hold it all
together.'

This 'poaching' can be seen most extensively in the painting
called *Time – Past and Present*. Three National Gallery paintings
are directly incorporated in the picture: Honthorst's *Saint
Sebastian* over the doorway, Zurbaran's *Saint Francis in Meditation*
to its left and, below this, part of Memlinc's *Saint Anthony Abbot*
from the back of the Donne triptych. But the principal source of
inspiration was the fifteenth-century artist Antonello da
Messina's panel of *Saint Jerome in his Study*.

'Saint Jerome by Antonello is the most magical painting – a house
within a church with Saint Jerome sitting there and, inside the church
but not quite inside his house, a little lion, running towards you from
the distance. It's a magical painting. Anyway, I wanted to do this old
friend of mine, Keith, as the saint, sitting in the room with all his
memories. Some of his memories are taken from pictures in the
National Gallery, and some of them are made up.'

Time – Past and Present is a picture that provides much material
for interpretation and speculation. The view through the door
originally showed a little boy playing outside on a tricycle. He
can still be seen in the small working drawings that were made

as part of the preparation for the painting. However, when the painting was almost finished he was suddenly painted out and replaced by the little girl who runs to greet the benign-looking old lady – who is perhaps this Saint Jerome's wife or housekeeper. Paula herself can't explain why this happened, except to say that 'in the end the picture has its own say.'

The picture of the sailor-boy on the wall and the model boat on the shelf provide clues that this Saint Jerome was once a sailor. The hippo, modelled from a toy hippo that Paula bought from a toy shop, is perhaps a memory of distant travels. The frightening-looking pictures above the shelf, with a fierce nun tightly gripping a smaller figure, represents a legend that Paula invented for this painting. 'It's a legend that I made up about a little girl from the sea, who eats up sailors. This Saint Jerome's brother was a sailor and was sacrificed to this girl from the sea by some nuns, who ran a school, and who were very strict.'

The contrasts between old and young, male and female, active and passive, all contribute to the curious mood of this picture. The old man nears the end of his life, and sits quietly and introspectively. The baby on the right is Paula's granddaughter Lola, who is at the start of her life, and may symbolise renewal, curiosity, or innocence.

The little artist girl seated on the left, who is about to begin a drawing, is in fact the artist in *Joseph's Dream*, although here she

Time – Past and Present.
Acrylic on paper laid on canvas,
183 x 183 cm.

Studies on paper for *Time – Past and Present*.

is much younger – this painting being the third in the sequence with *Joseph's Dream* the fourth. 'She's doing a secret drawing,' Paula says. 'I didn't want to put a drawing there, or you could see what she was doing. I didn't want anybody to see it, because it's too secret.' It is as if Paula herself does not know what the little girl is drawing, as if the characters that she invents have lives of their own, secret even from their creator. This little girl, though, provided the momentum for the next painting, because she grows up to become the young woman artist in *Joseph's Dream* – the painting closest to a National Gallery picture, being modelled on Philippe de Champaigne's *Vision of Saint Joseph*.

Watching the Old Masters entering Paula's paintings is a fascinating business. In *The Bullfighter's Godmother* there is hardly a hint, but in *The Fitting*, Steen and Mantegna creep in. In *Time – Past and Present* the way that Paula constructs a picture suddenly changes, with the discovery of the relevance of Renaissance perspective to her procedures. It is here, also, that we find the first direct quotes – from Honthorst, Zurbaran and Memlinc. Finally, in *Joseph's Dream* we see a National Gallery painting 'unpainted' so to speak, and then repainted by a new artist. But who is really painting that picture? Is it Paula Rego or the artist she has invented? Whatever the answer, Paula's work from the National Gallery paintings has extended their meaning still further, and it is perhaps best to end with her own description of that remarkable collection: 'A treasure house . . . it's all treasure of the greatest kind, the richest treasure in the world.'

Crivelli's Garden.
Acrylic on canvas, 190 x 240 cm.

The two paintings reproduced here are part of a series of three, the third of which was unfinished at
the time of writing. They are designed to be hung together and are entitled *Crivelli's Garden*.
A selection of studies and drawings for this project is included in this exhibition.

Crivelli's Garden (The Visitation).
Acrylic on canvas, 190 x 260 cm.

Carlo Crivelli (active 1457-93) was an Italian painter who specialised in altarpieces depicting the lives of the saints. The figures in Paula's pictures all represent the various saints found in National Gallery paintings, gathered together in one fictional place, Crivelli's garden.

Carlo Crivelli, *Altarpiece: The Virgin and Child with Saint Jerome and Saint Sebastian,* c.1491-2.
Wood (poplar), main panel 150.5 x 107.5 cm.

On viewing Paula Rego

Germaine Greer

WRITING of Paula Rego's work in 1987, her late husband, Victor Willing, reminded us that romance is not born but made. How it is made is the artist's secret. What we observe, in whatever medium, is the drama that results when she has created her scene and filled it with an action of her own devising.

The word 'character' originally meant, and fundamentally means, a sign. Paula Rego's painted characters signify as written characters do. They first exist as calligraphy, showing the impress of her own imagination and personality in the rhythm of their movement on the picture plane, and then as hieroglyphs that we can read. Some of them are ideograms, which carry within their shape a reminder of shapes connected with their primary meaning; others are pictograms as well. All the signs function on more than one level.

It is the tension between these functions that creates Paula Rego's irony, just as it is the tension between what is on the canvas and what is in the picture that is the great excitement of painting. A painting is clearly flat, and we must never forget the fact, but at the same time we must be lured into it and consent for the time we stand before it to become part of its world. We

Studies for *Crivelli's Garden* and *Crivelli's Garden (The Visitation)*.
Pen and ink and acrylic on paper, 30 x 40 cm.

must register what is painted at the same time that we register how it is painted. Often Paula Rego's figures, themselves chimeras, stand backlit before a luminous void. Our eye is drawn beyond them to the most romantic realm of all, the unknown.

Though we feel that within the picture we recognise shapes and motifs, at the same time we are obliged to register their strangeness. Soft is expressed in terms of hard, or solid in terms of transparent. Heavy things float and light things seem glued to the ground. Figures loom over us, topple towards us, the floor upon which they stand seems giddily raked up like a stage or falls away from us. The representational language has been subverted; the picture frame itself is undermined.

Traditionally the creativity of women has not chosen to express itself inside picture frames. Women's *poesis* has worked through other media nowadays disdained or commercialised. Historically the vast mass of female graphic and plastic production was biodegradable. Either it was eaten, or worn until it rotted, or carried to the well once too often. For special celebrations village women in India still paint wonderful patterns with dense symbolic significance in white lime on the trodden red earth threshholds of their houses; by the end of the holy day the sacred designs are no more. It took the tourist commission to degrade these vanishing designs by imprisoning them in black ink on white paper and selling them for money. The creation of monuments, whether two dimensional or three, has been an overwhelmingly masculine affair. In Western culture for the last thousand years or so women have been the consumers of male prowess; they have provided the applause and the adulation, in return for the idealisation of their own imagery that was at once their glory and their burden.

When a woman consciously separates her creativity from the unsynthesised manifold by fixing it and framing it, she is challenging a masculine tradition. She is prompted by love and admiration for what men have done, and she confronts special problems in making her own drama. Imitation is the sincerest flattery and many women have been content to paint in the style of their masters so well that their work cannot now be distinguished from the work of their fathers and brothers. It is not possible to paint and to reject painting. What the greatest women painters have done when they dared to commandeer a flat framed space for themselves is to suggest their otherness by acts of creative subversion. If we look at the work of Artemisia Gentileschi or Judith Leyster we become aware of something disturbing; at the most obvious level we can see that their female bodies are not simply shape and surface. They have weight and bones. They jostle in the picture frame and do not lie 'like Danaë to the stars'. Neither Gentileschi's nor Leyster's irony was understood. Paula Rego is working now in an environment which should begin to grasp the nature of the female commentary upon the male tradition. We should now realise that the unsentimental is not bitter, strident or unfemale.

Selection of studies on paper for *Crivelli's Garden*.

In Rego's hands the idealised female form undergoes humanisation. It no longer floats but lurks or squats or shoves. *The Fitting* is an ironic commentary on every great female portrait there ever was, with particular reference to Goya and Velázquez, Modigliani and Balthus. The attendant on the right, whose shape is both more voluptuous and more unlikely than that of the belle, looks sceptically into the mirror. The attendant on the left looks as if she could blow the skirt up like a bellows and blast her client into beauty. The girl herself stands as if lost in a dream of her own loveliness, while her great dress boils around her like molten rock. When it solidifies she will either be trapped inside it or pop out of the top of it like a larva from an egg. Again the eye is anxiously out of the canvas to the unknown; we no more know what she really looks like than we know how we look ourselves. When we look back again, we wonder if the large monumental group is not the dream of the tiny girl figure smiling in her sleep in the corner of the armchair (self-pleasuring, narcissistic), or is she an effigy, the doll of the dream of the heavy-armed girl in the overwhelming frock? Irony is the art of suggesting alternatives.

The figure of the painter in *Joseph's Dream*, too, is charged with ironic reference. We think of Vermeer on his dais at the same time that we notice that this female figure's skirt, the counterpart of Vermeer's gadrooned breeches, is made of rock that balloons in a way that rock cannot. The tiny joint stool half-hidden by it seems sharp as a knife blade. The intentness of the

36

Studies for *Crivelli's Garden* and *Crivelli's Garden (The Visitation)*.
Acrylic on canvas, 80 x 100 cm.

painter's gaze, like the timeless contemplation of an Easter Island head, invades the sleeping man's vulnerability. The canvas seems to loom over him like a slab over a sepulchre, held up by the angel who tumbles towards the painter as if to hail her conception.

When Paula Rego talks about her work, she does not talk like this but in images. For her the images are the meaning. When a writer describes what is going on in a painting, she is translating it into a different kind of experience. The justification is that Rego's work invites the viewer to bring her own frame of reference. The act of not-quite recognition is an element in the painterly construction. In *Time – Past and Present* we must see at once that the painter of *Joseph's Dream* has dwindled; she is now small and androgenous. Though the male subject is still oblivious of her, now he is invulnerable and dwarfs her. She does not look at him but at her blank paper, shielding it from his eyes with her arm, as if hoping to find her own imagery springing fresh and new on the page, but the page remains blank. He is Saint Jerome confined in his cell, but his cell is constructed of powerful images of a wandering past. As his past is the only past there is, it is perforce her past too. The polyptych of archetypal images that is their interior space draws our eyes towards a space beyond, just as luminous as the painter's paper, where there flickers a tiny ikon of life and love. We find the same glow and the same suggestion made manifest in the gaze of the baby emerging as if from a cocoon.

The fantasy scenarios that one might write, the dialogue that one might imagine for a scene like *The Bullfighter's Godmother* are relevant. They can be neither right nor wrong. Godmother is also God the mother, the mother god, the mother of gods and the mother of God, the Madonna. She wears a riding habit that pushes at the matador and Mrs Thatcher shoes that make her taller than him as she fixes him with her glittering eye. Can the contemplating painter have turned into a marionette mistress? Here we have no massive old man, but a young man in his prime. How can he seem so vulnerable, so overwhelmed? The little girl in the armchair may know, but she has the same dreaming look as the girl trying on the ballgown in *The Fitting* and the smile of the sleeper in that other armchair. The chair opposite is Saint Jerome's chair; the garment on it like Saint Jerome's jacket retains the form of the body that once filled it. Again we have a feeling of a chrysalis split open, of things becoming rather than being.

It is inevitable that a painter like Paula Rego working within the context of a great international art collection would illustrate the story of her own love affair with the tradition. We all share that love affair, and the same trepidation when it comes to finding our own creative language. Very few of us will ever know how Rego constructs her magic spaces, where smooth and rough and dark and bright dance as tensely as any flamenco. She will be content if our imaginations shed their timidity and join in.

PAULA REGO

1935
Born in Lisbon

1945-51
Educated St Julian's School, Carcavelos

1952-6
The Slade School of Art

1957-63
Lived in Ericeira, Portugal, with her husband
the painter Victor Willing

1962-3
Bursary from the Gulbenkian Foundation, Lisbon

1963-75
Lived in London and Portugal

1976
Settled permanently in London

1983
Visiting Lecturer in Painting, Slade School of Art

1988
Retrospective Exhibition, Gulbenkian Foundation, Lisbon
Serpentine Gallery, London

1990
Appointed the first National Gallery Associate Artist